1.9.88

THE STORYTELLER OF MARRAKESH

In the Djemaa el Fna, the central square of Marrakesh, sits the storyteller. For a few coins he will entertain you with tales of magic and fantasy, of humour and instruction. Many of the stories are folk tales of the Berber people, a race which settled in what is now Morocco over 1000 years ago. Though the Berbers have their own spoken languages, their written language is Arabic. The stories are akin to the Arabian Nights, with their djinns and ghouls, but also have the flavour and atmosphere of a people who are mainly engaged in trading.

THE STORYTELLER OF MARRAKESH

Based on traditional tales
from Morocco told by
Ahmed Benchaga to Tony Barton
Illustrations by Helen Backhouse

Evans Brothers Limited
London

First published 1980 by Evans Brothers Limited,
Montague House, Russell Square, London WC1B 5BX.

British Library Cataloguing in Publication Data

Barton, Tony
The storyteller of Marrakesh. – (Evans fables series).
I. Title
823′.9′1J PZ8.2

ISBN 0-237-45505-6

PRA 6829
Photoset by Northampton Phototypesetters Ltd.
Printed and bound in Great Britain by
William Clowes (Beccles) Limited, Beccles and London

Contents

For Daniel and Thomas, my first audience.

The Man in the Circle

The drums woke Ahmed.

Every afternoon towards five o'clock, when the noon heat began to cool, the drums woke people all over Marrakesh.

Ahmed rose from his low bed and pulled on a djellaba – *the long, loose white robe worn in his country, Morocco. He went on soft bare feet to the door of his room, and opened it just a crack. No one must hear him leave the house.*

At once he heard his father's voice, talking with his friends, lazily in the shaded courtyard of their house. His mother would be in her room still. She liked to rest a long time. He pulled the door all the way open, and

walked quietly from his room. He smiled to himself as he passed along the balcony over his father's head, carrying his sandals. He knew that if his father saw him, he would make him read some boring school book. But Ahmed had a better plan.

He reached the street without being seen, put on his sandals and began to run. He ran between the tall houses, dodging his way round all the people. They walked slowly in the same direction. Ahmed knew that they were going to the same place as he was himself – the Djemaa el Fna.

He bumped into someone, and he nearly fell. But it was no one he knew. So he saved himself and ran on. He ran past the sellers of vegetables and fruit and

flowers; the coppersmiths tap-tapping away at their work; the rug merchants with brightly coloured rugs pinned to the walls of their shops. In one street he ran under great thick hanging loops of wool – red, orange, yellow. The wool would soon be made into more rugs.

But at last the Djemaa el Fna opened out in front of him. It was the central square of the city – a huge open space, paved over, where people from far and near came to walk, sit, talk, listen, sell and sometimes to buy.

From the square you could look up to see the snowy Atlas Mountains. Ahmed thought of the little house where his grandmother lived, high up in those mountains among the great forest trees. He liked going there. Life was so different up in the mountains, like people used to live long ago, before our modern world of machines and television began to spread to every country.

Ah! There they were, the people he had come to find! Groups of people stood in an open part of the square, talking to each other. They looked as if they were waiting for someone. Ahmed knew who it was. More and more people joined these groups, making one big circle.

Then all of a sudden, there he was, Halaiki, the man in the circle. A tall man, though old now, he carried a stick, and he waved it in greeting to the circle of people. Many voices called out greetings in return, as they sat down to be ready for him. They knew him well, and came every day to hear him, for Halaiki was a man who told stories to anyone who cared to listen to him. This was how he made a living. At the end of each day he would collect money from his listeners. If the story was a good one, and he had told it well, they were generous. Sometimes his stories went on for many days, weeks even. Sometimes they were quite short.

Ahmed had been coming for several days now, whenever he could get out of the house. His parents thought that listening to Halaiki was a waste of time for a well-educated boy like Ahmed. Most of the listeners were poor people who could not read stories for themselves. But Ahmed loved the stories.

When Halaiki swished his stick through the air, describing a sword-fight, Ahmed would duck his head in fright. Around the circle the other heads ducked too. He held his breath at the ghoul who ate human flesh, and all around him many other breaths were sucked in too. Another time, Halaiki would make them all laugh to fill the Djemaa el Fna with the sound.

Today, Ahmed was lucky. He found a little empty place at the front of the circle, sat down with crossed legs, and raised his head, all ready to listen.

Halaiki held up his stick for silence.

"Today, my friends," he began, "and perhaps tomorrow too, we will follow the adventures of a boy who was born very poor. He had nothing. No education, not even a father to help him on in life. He had only honesty, and a wish to work hard."

He paused, and looked all round the circle. At last he pointed his stick at Ahmed, which made the boy hide his face for a moment. "But sometimes, my young friend," he went on, smiling, "sometimes such things are enough for one man."

Khalid the Dreamer

In the great forests of the Atlas Mountains there once lived a widow and her young son, Khalid. He was a hard-working boy and as he grew up it was found he was very clever with all growing things. In a little plot of land beside their log-hut, he grew all manner of fine vegetables and fruits, and the plants seemed almost to obey him. The widow and her son, though they were very poor, always had enough to eat from their garden. Sometimes they had enough to sell some of the food, and earn a little money to buy other necessary things, like shoes and warm clothes for the winter. But it was known that if a poor beggar went to his door, Khalid would always find something for him to eat.

The other people of the village came to admire the well-kept garden, where the results of Khalid's hard work were open for all to see. Khalid himself was as open and honest as his tidy rows of vegetables.

Now Khalid was glad that his skill as a gardener made an honest living for his mother and himself. But all the same he could not stop himself dreaming of other worlds, other lives.

Other boys, he knew, sometimes had bad dreams about the ghouls and djinns of the forest, and some even said they had seen the King of the Forest riding with his men all dressed in black robes right through the side of a mountain. But Khalid's day-dreams were always of a beautiful world of palaces and kings and rich clothes and brave heroes and lovely princesses. He knew very well that there was no place for a humble gardener in such a world, but that did not stop him dreaming.

When he sat, in the evening, keeping the birds off his young plants with a stick, the dreams would always come. There was one which came nearly every evening. In it he saw a beautiful Princess so clearly that he came to believe that it must be the Princess who, people said, was the daughter of the great King in the city below the mountains.

But in the morning he always returned to the work in his garden. He never let his dreams make him forget the attention his plants needed to grow strong and bear crops.

It happened one year when Khalid was a well-grown young man that a rich merchant rode through his village and rested there. He heard talk of the honest young gardener, and as he himself had a big garden at his home in the city below the mountains, he was interested to see what Khalid was doing.

The rich man saw at once that Khalid was no ordinary gardener, and he said to himself, if this young man could make my garden as fine as this, it would be a very good thing for me.

So there and then he asked Khalid to come to work for him.

Khalid and his mother went with the merchant to the great city, and they were given a little house to live in just by the garden wall. The merchant looked after them very well, and in return Khalid soon made the garden grow so much that it produced twice as much as before. They were very happy there.

Now that he was working for a rich man, Khalid was able to try out different kinds of plants that he had not grown before. Soon he had filled the gardens with colourful flowers and sweet-scented bushes. The merchant was very pleased and let him plan the gardens as he wished. They became known through all the city.

Khalid still had day-dreams in which he saw the same lovely Princess. Even though he had done so well in his new job, the beautiful world he saw inside his own head seemed just as far from his reach. But perhaps, now that he lived in the city, he might one day catch a glimpse of the Princess.

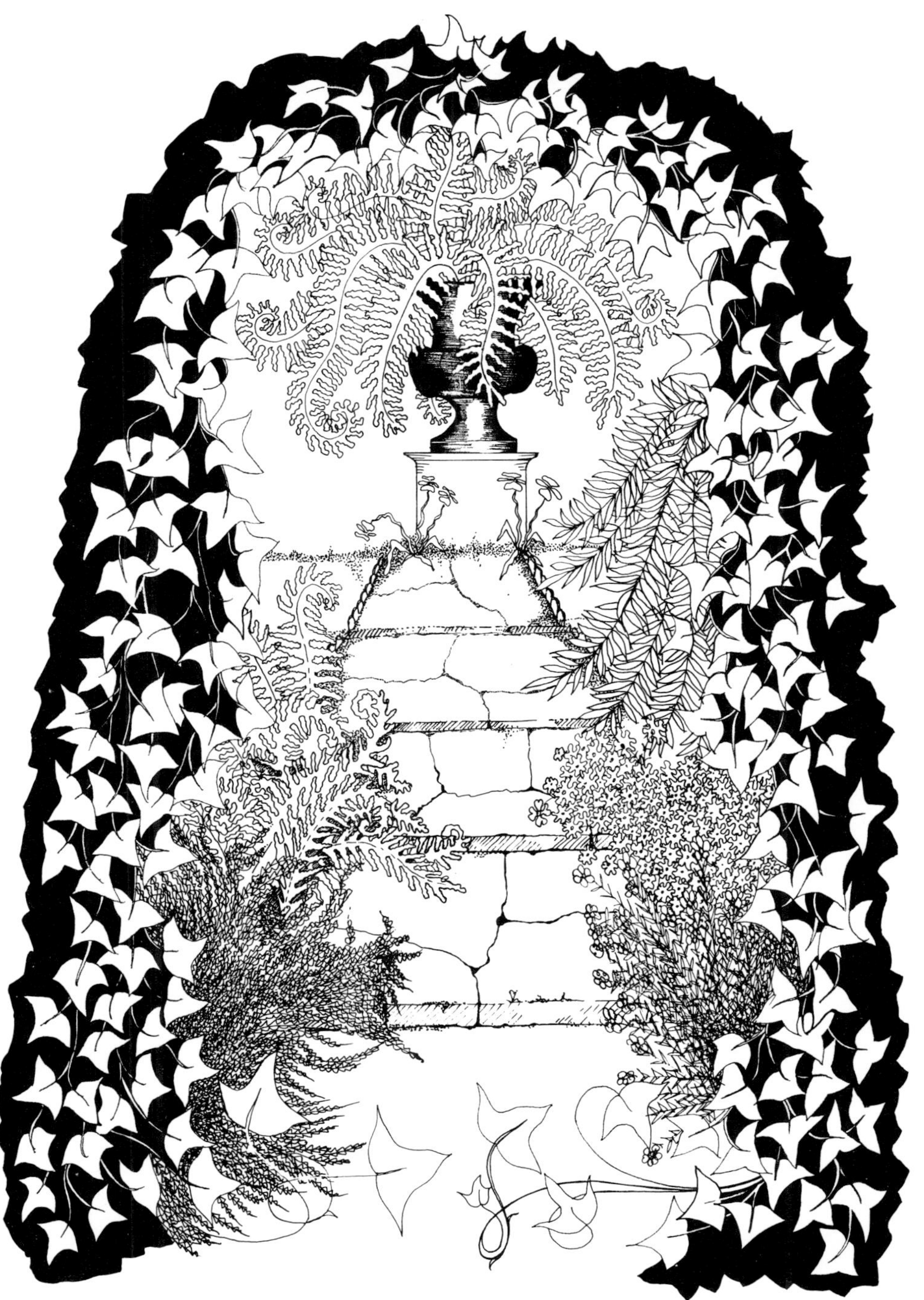

One evening, as he worked at the cool time of the day, he heard some strange sounds coming from a clump of bushes. He heard voices and laughter, but it did not sound like any laughter he had heard before.

He tiptoed carefully across a path, and parted the branches quietly with his hands. There he saw a party of strange little men, dancing and playing happily among themselves. He watched them for a while, keeping very quiet. Though he was curious to know who they were, he went home to his mother, without speaking to them.

Later that night, after the sun had set and a clear silver moon lit the whole gardens, there was a knock on his door. When he opened it, there were the dwarfs he had seen before.

"Please," they said, "the catch on the garden gate is too high for us. Will you let us out now?"

Filled with wonder, Khalid did so, and they skipped off happily. He turned to go indoors, but as he walked back along the path, he saw something bright on the ground, shown up by the moonlight.

He picked it up and saw that it was a shining jewel of some kind.

He showed it to his mother.

"It must be valuable," she said. "If you take it to the market-place tomorrow, you can sell it for a lot of money."

So Khalid went to the market-place next morning, and found a merchant of precious stones. He had never seen a jewel before, and had no idea how much to ask for it. So when the crafty dealer offered him ten dinars, that seemed a good price to him and he took the money home to his mother. They spent the evening planning what they should buy with it, and talking about their good luck.

But, at the same time as the night before, when the moon was high, there was a little knock on their door and Khalid found all the dwarfs standing outside, looking very unhappy and worried.

"Why, what is the matter?" asked Khalid. "Yesterday you all seemed so happy!"

"We have lost our jewel. It is our most precious thing," they said. "We wondered if you had seen it during your work in the garden."

Now here was a terrible thing! For a moment, Khalid could not think of anything to say to them. But he pulled himself together, and knew there was only one thing to be done.

"Yes, I know where your jewel is," he said, "but it is not here now. If you will come tomorrow night, I will have it for you."

The dwarfs were very pleased and happy again, and agreed to knock on his door the next night.

He let them out of the garden as before, and prayed that the jeweller would have kept the stone.

The next day he went to the shop and explained that there had been a mistake. He showed the ten dinars to the man, and asked for the jewel back.

The man laughed. "My good fellow," he said, "what a tale to bring to an honest man! I've never seen you before and as for a valuable jewel, what would a poor gardener like yourself know of any such thing?"

Khalid argued with him, but it was no good. The crafty dealer insisted there had been no jewel and the ten dinars were nothing to do with him.

"What is all this story?" said a voice behind Khalid. He turned to see a beautiful young lady, very richly dressed, with two servant-girls beside her, standing in the doorway of the shop.

The jeweller changed his manner at once. He bowed low and his voice was all politeness.

"Oh your Highness, it is nothing, just this ignorant young gardener . . ."

The lady interrupted him. "I don't believe a word of it," she said. "I know you too well. Give him back his jewel this minute. He looks honest to me." Though she said this, she had not given Khalid more than a passing glance.

"Yes, your Highness," said the jeweller, with a wicked look at Khalid. All the same, he reached into a pocket and brought out the dwarfs' bright stone. He had to press it into Khalid's hand, and take the ten dinars from his fingers. Khalid was gazing at the beautiful girl.

He had seen her twenty – no, a hundred – times before and he stood struck dumb with amazement. Could this be the Princess of his dreams?

But the Princess, for that is who it was, had turned her attention to some ear-rings the jeweller had for her. Neither the royal customer nor the clever dealer had any more interest in the gardener.

When the tiny knock came on Khalid's door, he went with the jewel in his hand and gave it to the dwarfs as he had promised. They were delighted and danced away with it in great happiness.

But Khalid and his mother, as you would expect, were not so happy. True, the jewel was not theirs, and they were no worse off than if they had not found it at all. But because of it, poor Khalid had seen the Princess. He thought he might never see her again. And if the Princess he had seen in his dreams had been far above him, then the real Princess, who had hardly looked at him in the shop, seemed so very much more out of his reach.

All the same, in the morning, the plants had to be looked after, Princess or no Princess, but Khalid went about his work with a heavy heart. When his master came to see him, as he did each day, he asked him why he looked so sad.

"Is there anything I can do for you?" he asked.

Then Khalid felt a little ashamed. He was lucky to have such a kind master who gave him plenty of work and a house to live in. So he tried to forget his sadness, and told his master he was not feeling very well, but he would soon be better.

In the evening, he heard the knock once more, and opened the door to the dwarfs. They were looking kindly at him and they said, "We have seen how sad you are today. We have a present for you."

They held out a small almond shaped piece of wood, polished smooth and fitting pleasantly into the palm of his hand.

"This wooden almond has magic powers. It will help you to beat all dangers. If you rub it with your fingers it makes music."

Khalid rubbed it gently and the air was filled with the most beautiful sounds of music. The dwarfs went away and he and his mother turned the wooden almond over and over in their hands.

"What can we do with it?" said his mother. "It will not buy us new shoes, will it? We should sell it and use the money."

Khalid did not like to sell the strange object which his friends the dwarfs had given him. But he obeyed his mother and went into the city next day.

He found a place in the square, and stood there rubbing the smooth wood and filling the streets around with wonderful music. First one, then two people looked round, and stopped to hear. They smiled as if the music made them happy. Soon a crowd gathered about Khalid.

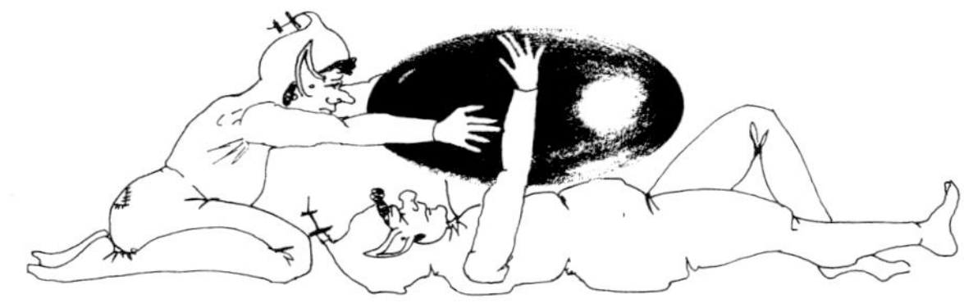

But to his surprise no one asked the price. Instead, they each threw small coins at his feet, as though to reward him for the pleasure he had brought them. He stood there all day, playing the music, and at the end of it had collected nearly three dinars. On the way home, he bought the shoes his mother wanted.

He returned next day and the same thing happened. For many days, he played music in the streets of the city and always he collected money.

Khalid now began to be known as widely for his music as he had been before for his gardening. Rich people asked him to come to their parties and play for the guests. At last the Princess in her palace heard of him and commanded her servants to fetch him to play for her.

So Khalid put on his best clothes. He went to the palace, and found in a great hall not only the Princess, but the King her father and a hundred guests. He played on his wooden almond and as before, everyone was enchanted with the music, which seemed to come from another world.

When he at last stopped playing, the Princess looked at him for a moment, then held out her hand. "I will buy it from you," she said.

Now although Khalid had meant to sell it at first, he did not know what to do. He thought the Princess very proud and also a little rude to him, but still he wanted to give her a pleasing answer.

The King saw that he was troubled, and in front of the big audience, himself offered to buy it for his daughter. He spoke kindly to Khalid.

Khalid at last said, "I will exchange this magic thing for the ring on your daughter's finger." That way at least he would have something by which to remember her.

The King and the Princess agreed to this exchange, and Khalid passed over the magic almond. But when the Princess tried to play the music herself, it remained silent. Not a note would it play for her. The King took it and also rubbed gently, with no better success.

Quietly he handed it back to Khalid, and at once the music burst forth again.

The King turned to his daughter and said, "My dear, if you want the music, you must have the musician too "

So Khalid was made court musician at the Royal Palace. He and his mother had a good house in the Palace grounds, and he said goodbye to his kind master, the merchant.

In his new job, Khalid felt that, at last, he was a part of the dream world of richly dressed and beautiful people he had thought he would never know. The King and the Princess always seemed to be giving large parties or receiving foreign kings and queens. Quite often rich princes came to seek the Princess's hand in marriage. But she was as grand and haughty with them as she was with everybody else. She would have none of them. The King her father was very worried about her, but he did not know what to do. Meanwhile, every day there was some grand event at which Khalid had to play his wonderful music. Khalid himself was happy at first just to be near the Princess.

But as time went by, he found that she was further away from him than ever. At least in his dreams they were always alone together and talked freely to each other. But the real Princess never spoke to him except to give him orders. She remained proud and treated him like a servant. But the King came to like Khalid, and was often kind to him when the Princess had said something hurtful.

Also Khalid began to miss his gardening. He used to love seeing the tiny seeds grow. First, they would peep above the soil, then timidly grow up towards the sun, and finally burst boldly into flower. Playing a musical instrument, even a magic one, left him feeling he was not doing anything really useful. It grew no one any food, and it certainly wasn't doing anything to make the Princess be kind to him.

It happened at that time that the King was fighting a war against another king. The palace was often full of soldiers back from the fighting, with stories of brave deeds and wild horse rides through the desert chasing the enemy. Khalid was amazed by these men, so bronzed and so tough, yet so laughing and light-hearted.

He thought he would like to be a soldier and go to the war.

He went to ask the Princess for permission to join up. With no pause for thought at all, she said, "No, of course not. What nonsense. I must have you here to play the music for me." And she would not even discuss it.

Khalid was very unhappy and thought about what to do. It seemed it was the wooden almond that now stood in his way. He decided to return to his old master's garden and seek the dwarfs' advice.

He found them there, at dusk, playing as usual. He explained his trouble to them. They said, "You must let us keep the magic music-maker for you. Whenever you need it again you shall have it if you come to us."

So he gladly handed it back to them. The next time the Princess sent for him to play for her, he told her he no longer had it.

The Princess was very angry. She wanted to have him put to death for, of course, she knew it was his way of disobeying her about going to the war. She commanded the palace guards to seize him, and she went to her father, the King.

"This man has thrown away his music-maker. I want him killed," she said.

The King was very shocked to hear this, but he did not let his daughter guess his thoughts. He said to her, "Very well, but let me send him to the war. That is what he wants so he will go gladly. I will have sent him against the enemy, and so he will die that way, and no one will think us cruel."

The Princess agreed to this plan, and Khalid said goodbye to his mother, and went off to the wars.

But the King gave orders that he was to be given the best soldier's training, and he sent after him a fine sword of the best steel to use as his own in battle. Khalid soon became a good soldier.

Halaiki broke off for a moment, and looked at the sky. His voice was tired as he said, "It grows late, we must finish this story tomorrow." He took a bag from inside his djellaba, *and began collecting his money.*

Ahmed wanted him to go on, to hear how Khalid got on as a soldier. But he knew that if he left it any later, he would have questions to answer at home. If they found out where he had been, they would stop him coming.

So he put into the bag the small coin he had brought especially, and ran off home. He let himself in, met no one, and went into the family evening meal without a word.

"I hope you have learned a lot from your schoolbooks today," said his father.

"Yes father, I have learned many things," said Ahmed, thinking to himself, "Well, it's true, though not from schoolbooks."

Next day, he slipped out as the drums began to beat, and arrived just in time to hear Halaiki begin again the story of Khalid.

Because it was wartime for that city, visitors no longer came to the palace. The Princess sometimes felt lonely, and she missed the evenings when Khalid made music on his magical wooden almond.

No news came from the war, and she did not know whether he was alive or dead. She was sorry now that she had been so angry. But she still would not ask her father about him. She began to be bored with the life she led.

One day when she looked out of her window early in the morning, she saw a richly dressed man on a horse draw up before the palace, and beside him ten men in long black robes. Each man carried a large golden box on his shoulders.

The leader was admitted to the King's hall, and bowing low he said, "Oh great King, I come from the King of the Forest. He sends these rich gifts to you, and begs for the hand of your daughter in marriage."

Now the King had heard no good of the King of the Forest. This strange King was said to use bad magic on his subjects. The thought of his beautiful daughter marrying such a man did not please our King at all. But there was no doubting the richness of the treasures in each box. Jewels and silks and gold and silver poured out of each one as it was opened.

The Princess, however, was very excited to see the splendid presents, and she begged her father to let her go to marry the King of the Forest. The more the King advized her against the idea, the more she wanted to go. She was obstinate, but he was afraid that later on she would be sorry she had done it.

At last he agreed, but against his will.

She made herself ready, and some days later she set off with the horseman and the ten black-robed men. She rode in a litter, with some maidservants of her own. They travelled a long and dusty way, and came to the edge of the forest just as the daylight was fading.

The sky was dark and stormy, and as they rested a moment before entering the forest, great rolling claps of thunder made them all bow their heads in fear. But the Princess would not let anyone see she was afraid. She held her head up as proudly as ever, even when her young servant maids ran screaming away to hide amongst the trees. The girls found a hut to hide in and waited there all night, till at dawn the storm seemed to have gone away.

They returned to where they had left their mistress. But the horseman, the ten men, the

Princess in her litter, had all gone.

Nowhere could they find the Princess.

The King of the Forest had taken her to his cavern kingdom under the ground. There he made her into a slave and gave her all the rough, dirty jobs to do.

Knowing nothing of what had happened to his daughter, the King went on with the war and at last his army seemed to be winning. One day Khalid came riding into the city at the head of the army and soon everyone had heard the good news. The war was over.

The King received his victorious Captains, and among them was Khalid. But what a different Khalid! Now he was bronzed and tough. His mother thought he looked more handsome than before. He had fought well and had led many men into battle. The King was so pleased to see him that he made him Captain of the Palace Guards, a position of high honour.

Khalid was very sad when he heard about the Princess going to marry the King of the Forest. If only she could have seen him now, he thought, perhaps she might have liked him more.

Then one of the Princess's maidservants came to the Palace gates. She had had a long and very weary journey to find her way back alone. She told them about the Princess and the storm. The King at once sent his men to the forest to look for his daughter. But they found nothing and came back almost afraid to speak of their failure. The King was very miserable and could not think of any way of finding her.

Khalid thought of his friends the dwarfs, and the magic almond they were keeping for him. He went to see them, and told them of his trouble. They at once gave him back the music-maker and said, "We know the King of the Forest. He is a bad man and has put the Princess under a spell. But if you go to the edge of the forest and wait till dark, you will see the ground open up. You must jump in then without being seen, and go to seek the Princess in the cavern kingdom. And remember, the magic music-maker will always protect you."

So Khalid went to the King and said, "Sire, I would like to try to find the Princess and save her from the King of the Forest. He has put her under a spell."

The King had always liked Khalid and he trusted him now. He wished him well, and Khalid set off, taking the fine sword the King had given him, and his magic wooden almond.

He made his way to the place where the maid had said she had last seen the Princess. He hid in a nearby tree and waited for the sun to set. As the great red disc sank out of sight, the whole sky darkened and a great noise like rumbling thunder filled Khalid's head. To his amazement, it came not from the sky, but out of the ground.

Suddenly a split showed in the earth. It grew wider and wider and some soldiers came marching out of it. Khalid slid down his tree and just as the soldiers went from sight into the forest, he jumped down into the huge hole. It closed over him with a mighty clang.

There was a little light, and he saw a wide passage stretching away before him, going into the earth. Carefully he went along it, till far ahead he could hear sounds of voices and laughter and much other noise. He came nearer and nearer till at last he could look round a huge rock.

He was at the edge of a very big cave. It was lit by hundreds of burning torches, which filled the place with their piny scent as they burned smokily. Through the thick air he saw many people, some moving, some still. The still ones were tall men in black robes, like the ones who had carried the treasure for the Princess. They stood around with long swords, guarding all the entrances to the cavern kingdom.

In the centre of the cave, there were men with huge glistening muscles wrestling with each other. To one side, a man was fighting a big black boar. The boar's tusks were covered with blood. In another part, three men held a lion by the tail, while three others fought it with long sharp sticks.

Many sports of this cruel kind were going on. But Khalid's eye was drawn to a high throne at the far side of the cavern.

The huge man sitting there, laughing and pointing at the scene before him was the King of the Forest. His skin was dark red, and he had a bushy black beard. He was surrounded by servants who held great plates of food from which he was picking the best pieces. Sometimes when one of the wrestlers made a good throw, he tossed a large lump of meat to him. Once he threw a whole sheep's leg to the lion.

Khalid pulled back his shoulders, put his hand on his sword and strode into the middle of the cavern. He was such a splendid figure in his rich robe and with his rare sword that the noise slowly stopped, and the fighting men stood still.

The King of the Forest stood up and roared, "Who is this who dares to interrupt our sports?"

"I am Khalid. I come to take the Princess."

For a moment the King of the Forest looked at him in amazement. Then he burst out laughing. He held out a hand to keep back his guards, who had started forward as if to seize Khalid.

"You have come to take back the Princess, have you? And if I say I won't let you? What will you do then? Fight all my men at once? See, friends, here is one who would fight and kill two hundred!"

Khalid did not lose his nerve.

"I have not come to fight two hundred, oh King," he said, "but only one." He drew out his sword with a swish of steel. "I will fight you for her!"

The King looked at him hard. Again he began laughing.

"Foolish man!" he roared out, as loudly as before. "Do you think I fight nobodies like you! Come, let's have Gargorah! He's the one you can fight. Clear a space now."

The men in the centre of the cavern all drew back and made a wide space. Into this ten men led

a huge bear tied with ropes. At a sign from the King of the Forest they loosed the ropes, and Khalid found himself looking up into the blazing red eyes, and long white fangs of Gargorah, the fighting bear.

The animal's paws were so long that they could strike at Khalid easily and still keep away from the point of his sword. Khalid said to himself, "My last moment has come. But I must die bravely."

The bear sniffed the smoky air, and looked around. Everyone was keeping out of sight. Only Khalid stood there. The bear took three steps towards him. He was getting ready to run at Khalid and crush him with one blow of his great paw.

Then Khalid thought of the dwarfs. He took the magic music-maker from his pocket and rubbed it gently.

The sweet music filled that underground place. The King of the Forest leaped down from his throne and shouted, "Don't listen. Cover your ears! Don't listen!"

But it was too late. The first few notes had charmed everyone in the cave, so that they could not resist it.

The bear stood still and cocked his head, listening. Then slowly he began to dance. Up went his left foot, up went his right foot. Down stamped his right foot, down stamped his left foot. Faster and faster, and then again faster still, he hopped and stamped and stumped. He jigged and skipped and leaped, he bounced around in circles. He spun around like a top – until his legs could not keep up with his body and he fell to the ground quite worn out.

Khalid looked around him. No one was to be seen. In the midst of the bear's dance, they had all dashed away. The King of the Forest had rushed after them, trying to stop them and bring them back. All was silent, except for the heavy breathing of the exhausted bear.

Khalid heard from somewhere far off the sound of a bird singing. He followed the sound, and it led out of the black and smoky cavern, down passages and steps to a little room.

There he saw the bird, sitting in a little golden cage, singing to the magic music Khalid was playing.

There also in the little room was the Princess. Khalid stopped playing and stared at her. What a change had taken place! Instead of the beautiful, proud Princess who had always spoken to him like a servant, there was only a girl in a dirty robe. Her hands were blackened, her skin was rough. She was pale and tired-looking. Her hair hung about her face, where before it had always been beautifully dressed and oiled and scented.

Khalid spoke to her. She paid no attention, seeming to be held still. He saw she was under a spell, so he rubbed the wooden almond once more.

The Princess raised her hands to her cheeks, and then stretched her arms, like one coming out of a long sleep. Then she saw Khalid, standing there, looking at her.

At first she could not look at him. He had never seen her before in this sad condition, and she was ashamed to remember how she had always spoken to him. But she was so glad to be free of the spell, and to see again someone from the time when she was happy, that she soon gave him her hand. He helped her up, and led her out of the cavern kingdom, and took her back to her father.

She soon bathed herself and changed her clothes.

She was once again the beautiful Princess that Khalid had known before. All the wicked King's spells had lost their power because of the dwarfs' magic.

But yet she was not quite the same Princess who had spoken so rudely to Khalid in the days gone by, and had even wanted him killed. She had suffered and been very unhappy in the power of the King of the Forest. She was no longer so proud and haughty, and she knew that Khalid had been very brave.

And so, with the blessing of the King, her good father, and amid the tears of happiness of Khalid's mother, they were married and lived to rule wisely and kindly over that kingdom.

"Now, my friends," began Halaiki next day. "I will tell you about another poor man." He looked sternly at Ahmed. "But do not think, young fellow, that everybody can do as this man did."

"Was he *honest and hardworking?" asked Ahmed.*

"You shall see," was the reply.

Sarsaur

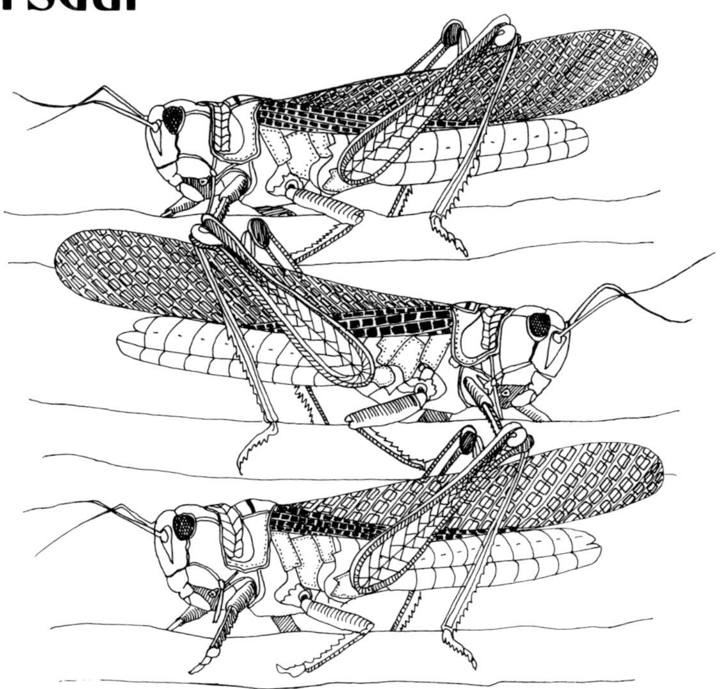

There was once in the land of the Atlas, a poor farm labourer called Sarsaur. Now Sarsaur, in the language of the people of the Atlas, means a grasshopper. He was small and skinny and his bones stuck out making him look all angles. Poor Sarsaur was not very clever and he never seemed to do very well.

One day he stood up from his work in the fields, his back aching. Talking aloud to himself was a curious habit of his, and he said to the empty air, "I'm so tired of this work. I work, work, work all day and I get no richer and still don't have three meals a day. If only . . . if only I had three good meals a day!" Wearily he went back to work.

After half-an-hour, he stood up again and talked some more to himself. "And I would like a decent house to sleep in, because I'm sore all over from sleeping on the floor." But so far as he could see, there was nothing to be done about it.

Some days later he went to market to sell what vegetables he had managed to grow. They were poor things and he didn't get much money from them. He looked at all the people there, selling things or getting money by amusing the crowds. He looked a long time at the magicians, who could tell you things, secret things, that were hidden from other people.

Back in his fields next day, he said aloud to himself, "All those fat tricksters you see in the market-place – they live just by their wits! They never dig, or hoe, or pull weeds. Yet they make more money than anyone else. Why can't I do that? I'm going to give up this life, and become a magician."

So there and then he dropped his tools and set off to seek his fortune as a magician.

He walked for a long time in the dusty roads, and got very hot and tired and hungry. He began to think that perhaps it was going to be more difficult to be a trickster than he had imagined. He saw only poor farm-workers like himself who had nothing to give him, even if he could trick them.

As he went on his way, worried about where he should stay for the night and what he should get for his supper, he came to a high mountain. Built into its rocky folds was a great *kasbah*. He knew this must be the home of a rich Prince. Perhaps here he might beg shelter and food, and who knows – trick somebody out of something?

He looked up at the tall square towers and wondered about the best way to get in to see the Prince. But as he trod wearily along under the sheer red walls, he heard on the other side a tremendous wailing and weeping, and one noise louder than all the rest. It was a woman crying.

He found the gate and asked a palace servant what was the matter. "Oh, my poor mistress the Princess has lost her most precious jewel. A fine ruby left her by her father, when he died. She used to love him very much, and whenever she looked at this ruby, she was reminded of him. And now she is very sad to have lost it. But she is also frightened."

"Why is she frightened?" asked Sarsaur. "Surely it's bad enough just losing it."

"Yes, but you see, when her husband the Prince comes home from his journey, she is afraid he will be very angry with her."

Sarsaur, thinking quickly, said at once, "I am a Magician, my good man. Let me in to speak to the Princess, and I will find the jewel for her."

The Princess's servant looked rather hard at Sarsaur, and it was obvious he didn't believe he could be a magician. He was dressed just like a poor farm labourer.

But he let him in, and led him through many courtyards to a shady garden, where fountains played and many beautiful bright birds flew about, dazzling the eye. Sarsaur thought there could be no more lovely place in the whole of Morocco.

In the midst of this paradise, however, the Princess sat sadly. So desperate was she that, even though Sarsaur looked just like any other poor peasant, she agreed to let him try to find the ruby. "What must we do, Oh Magician," she said, "to find my beautiful ruby?"

Now Sarsaur, as you may guess, didn't know any more than she did how he was going to find the ruby. So he pretended to think by closing his eyes, and holding his hand to his brow. At last, he said, "Great Princess, I have travelled far and am very tired. If you will give me three good meals I will certainly be able to find this jewel for you." You see, he reckoned that even though they would punish him when he proved unable to find the ruby after all, the three meals would be worth it.

The Princess at once gave orders for him to be taken to the guest house of the Palace. He was seated on a fine divan, his feet were washed in lovely cool water, and he was given delicious drinks while he waited for the food to be prepared.

His mouth was watering so much that by the time a servant girl entered with the food, he could think of nothing else but the three meals he had been promised. He said aloud to himself, forgetting that he wasn't in his empty fields, and that he would sound silly to the servant, "This is the first."

The food was like no other food he had ever tasted before. There were rich meats cooked in

spices and herbs and flavoured with lemon. There were melt-in-the-mouth sweets of almonds and honey, and there was some most refreshing mint tea. He ate and drank everything he could, and lay back to sleep it off, dreaming that this was what heaven must be like.

Some hours later, another servant girl came in carrying a tray full of delicious food, and Sarsaur again spoke aloud, "This is the second."

Yet a third time the food was brought as he had been promised, and he said aloud to himself, "This is the third."

He sank back into the most beautiful sleep, having quite forgotten what he was there for and why he had been given the meals.

He was woken next time by the three servant girls coming up to him all together, and looking most terribly frightened.

"Oh Great Magician," they all said together, "we are indeed the three guilty ones. You have found us out. We stole the ruby, but we pray to you on our knees not to tell the Princess. She will beat us and throw us out and we shall go hungry and probably die."

Sarsaur looked at them stupidly, still only half-awake. Then it all came back to him in one horrible rush. He tried to look clever and said, "How did you know I had found you out?"

"But you said to each of us, this is the first, this is the second, this is the third."

Sarsaur could hardly believe his good luck. But he took pity on the three girls, because he knew only too well what it was to be hungry. He thought hard how to trick the Princess into thinking he had found the ruby by magic, without getting them into trouble.

At length he asked them, "Where does the Princess spend her time?"

"With her collection of birds in the garden."

"So!" said Sarsaur importantly. "Fetch me a peacock."

They went out and came back with a peacock.

"Give me the jewel!" he commanded sternly, stretching out his open palm. Obediently they gave it to him, and he stuffed it down the unlucky bird's throat.

"Now put the peacock back with the other birds, and take me to the Princess."

The poor lady had been waiting impatiently for him and at once asked him, "Have you found it? Do you know where it is? Oh, please, please tell me?"

Sarsaur looked at the Princess, and said proudly, "Let your whole collection of birds parade before me, like an army under review, and I will promise

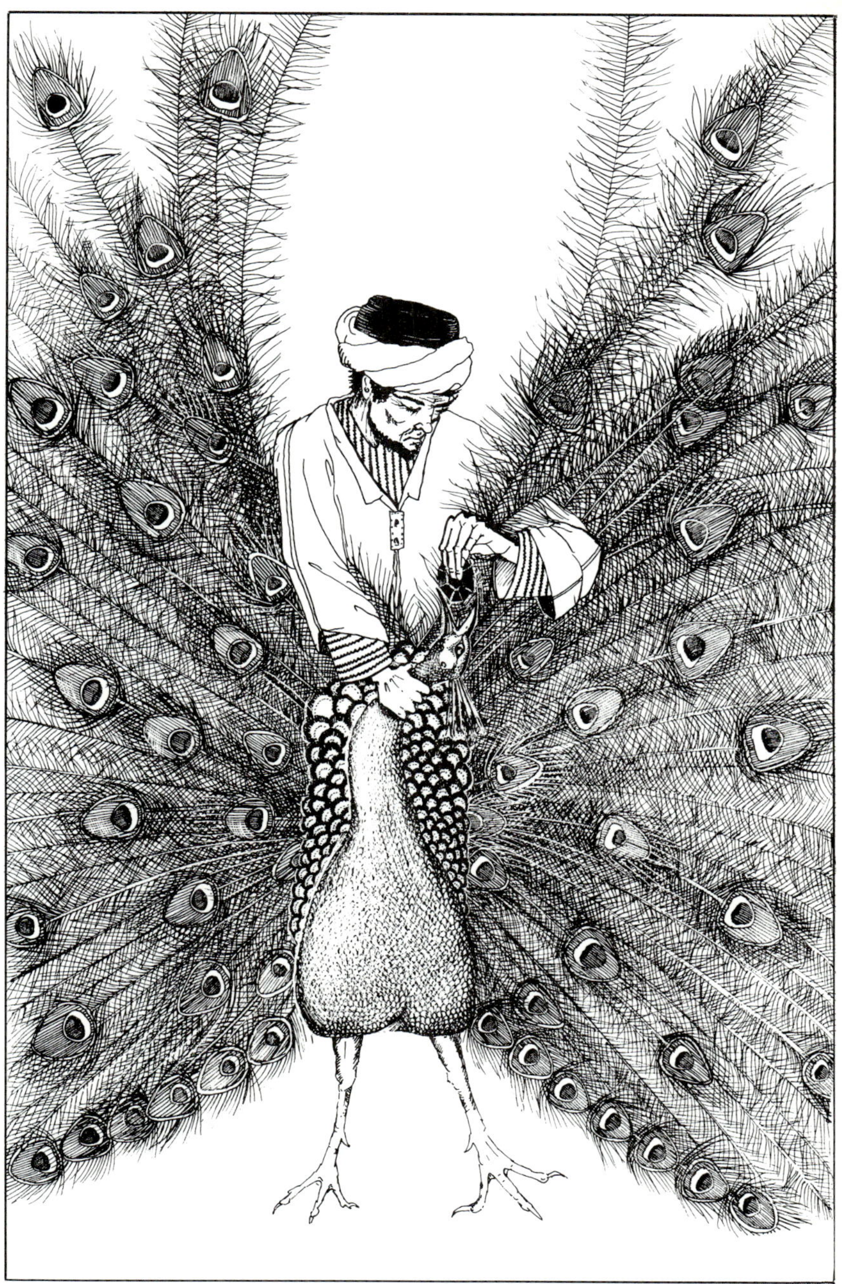

the ruby shall be in your hands immediately."

The Princess at once gave orders for the birds to be brought and one by one, sometimes two by two, all the birds marched past Sarsaur and the Princess. Everyone in the palace had gathered round to see, from the Prince's most important men to the smallest son of the doorkeeper.

There were an awful lot of birds, and as more and more came by, and Sarsaur did nothing, the Princess and all the people began to look sideways at Sarsaur, frowning.

But when the peacock came strutting by, Sarsaur pointed a terrible finger at him. "There is your thief!" he thundered.

The peacock was seized and cut open, and there was the bright red ruby in his crop.

Everyone present, the Prince's advizers and the palace guards – and especially the three servant girls, gasped at the Magician's cleverness and clapped their hands in admiration.

The Princess was overcome with joy and relief, and held the ruby to her breast, promising never to let it out of her sight ever again. Sarsaur she thanked and poured gold pieces into his hands, and insisted on his changing into fine clothes of silk and satin. She said he could stay in the palace and be the Court Magician.

"At last," said Sarsaur aloud to himself, as he settled down to sleep that night on his wonderfully soft divan. "At last, three meals a day! A luxurious bed to sleep on for the rest of my life. And all I had to do for it was eat all that marvellous food!

What a fool I was all those years to go on working so hard when it's so easy to be a magician!"

He fell asleep completely happy.

Next day the Prince came home. He was told the whole amazing story by his wife. He sent for Sarsaur and sat looking at him for a long time, saying nothing.

But Sarsaur did not like his looks one little bit. The Prince seemed to be thinking to himself that this Magician was only a trickster who had somehow fooled his wife. With a wave of his hand he sent Sarsaur away again, and said to the Princess, "I don't believe it, my dear. This is some low peasant who has tricked you."

"But I promise you it is all true. Ask anyone here," she said.

"I want some proof I can see for myself," said the Prince. "Give me a hat, any hat," he asked his chief advizer.

The hat was brought, and the Prince said, "Catch some small creature in the garden and put it under the hat."

So a man went out, and the first small creature he saw was a grasshopper. He caught it and took it back to the Prince and it was placed under the hat.

"Now send for this Magician again," said the Prince.

When Sarsaur was led back into the room once more, the Prince said, "Now let us see for ourselves what your magic is like. Tell me what is under that hat."

Sarsaur gazed at the hat, terrified. What had he landed himself into now? Oh what a fool, why hadn't he been content with the little he had had before he set out on this ill-fated journey?

He was so worried that he spoke aloud to himself, "You're really trapped this time, my friend Sarsaur!"

The Prince overheard the last word, and since, as you know, Sarsaur is the word in his language for Grasshopper, his face changed and he looked at the Magician in wonder.

"Why yes," he said, "it *is* a grasshopper." He lifted the hat, and the little creature jumped away out into the garden again.

So it came about that Sarsaur was indeed certain of three meals a day and a beautiful soft bed for ever afterwards.

"So, my boy," said Halaiki to Ahmed, "have I answered your question?"

Ahmed smiled. "Well, I think it was that Sarsaur was lucky, more than he was hard-working."

The circle laughed a little at this. Halaiki laughed too. "You are quite right. So much sense in one so young! Tell me your name."

"I am called Ahmed."

"Ahmed! That's a good name for a story! As we have plenty of time tonight, I shall tell you about Prince Ahmed, and the terrible ghoul who ate human flesh."

Prince Ahmed

In a great *kasbah* of the High Atlas mountains lived a young Prince called Ahmed. He led a happy and untroubled life with his mother, who loved him dearly, and his father, who was very proud of his strong body and his fearless character.

But Prince Ahmed began to be troubled by a very strange thing; each morning when he awoke he would find a spot of henna rubbed into the palm of his hand. He washed it clean and went off to his studies, but next morning there it would be again, and he could not think how it came there.

His schoolmaster was a very wise man and sensed that something was wrong with his young pupil.

But he said nothing until one day he noticed some stains of henna on the Prince's hand. Now henna is a red dye used mostly in that country by women, and by a man only on his wedding night. Puzzled, the old man asked, "Why are you using henna on your hand?"

Prince Ahmed didn't quite know what to say, for fear that he would not be believed. But at last he explained what was happening. The old schoolmaster didn't laugh at him, but regarded him thoughtfully.

"Well, my boy," he said at last. "Someone is putting that henna on your hand while you are asleep each night. It doesn't get there by itself. Here is what I suggest you do. Before you go to bed tonight, make a little cut on your hand, in the place where the henna is usually put. When this mysterious person comes to put on the henna, it will sting you and you will be awakened."

Prince Ahmed followed these instructions the same night. He had no trouble making the cut in his palm, because he was a brave young man, used to hard exercise and man's work when he went hunting. He lay down to sleep wondering what strange person he should meet that night.

When his hand began to sting he awoke to see a beautiful young girl busy rubbing henna into his palm. Quickly he seized her by the wrist and demanded, "Who are you? What do you want?"

"Let me go," she cried out instantly.

"Not until you tell me what you want and why you are doing this!"

The girl shook her head and replied, "No, you would not be able to afford my demands."

Prince Ahmed knew that his father, besides being a rich man, would refuse him nothing, so he pressed and pressed the girl to tell him what her demands were. The more she refused, the more he felt he wanted to keep her beside him so that he might see her every day.

At last she agreed to speak. "We can be together only if you build me a house where I may live unknown to your family behind seven iron doors."

The Prince at once agreed to this, thinking it was not so difficult after all. He had the house built, and the seven doors were fitted with seven locks. He visited the girl every day and they were very happy together.

But he began to neglect his studies, and he did not bother to see his mother each day as he had been used to. She wondered what had come over her son, and determined to find out what it was he did in the house he had persuaded his father to have built for him. But Ahmed always carried the keys about with him, and slept on them at night.

It chanced one day he went out hunting and left the keys buried in the stables. The busybody of the stableyard, the cockerel, scratched them up and at once began crowing over his find. A servant came to discover what the noise was, and saw the keys. This servant was a crafty fellow, and knew they must be the keys his mistress was so anxious to get hold of.

He went to Prince Ahmed's mother and said, "If you will give me a reward, I'll get your son's keys for you."

"Very well," she said. "Your reward will be to lick the dishes clean after the family has eaten."

He agreed to this, and the mother took the keys and unlocked the seven iron doors. As soon as she saw the girl, she was furious. She spoke to her very angrily, accusing her of taking her son from her, and making bitter insults. But at last she ran out of breath and went away to recover.

The girl did nothing until evening, when Prince Ahmed came back from hunting and went to see her.

"You have broken your promise and given the keys to your mother," she accused him, and nothing he could say would make her believe him. To his grief, she suddenly changed into a pigeon and flew out of the window.

Prince Ahmed was in despair. She had taken all of his happiness with her. He determined to follow the pigeon straightaway and see if he could find

his beautiful companion once more. He would not stay to listen to his mother, but took food for his journey, saddled a strong horse, and rode off in the direction the bird had taken.

As he had not started until late in the day, it was soon dark. He found himself in a great forest of pine-trees, where it was dark and gloomy. But through the dim twilight he heard the sound of children's voices, and he came upon two little boys who were searching for pine-nuts to chew. They were very dirty and tired, and obviously very hungry. Prince Ahmed knew they must be ghoul-children to be wandering about like this at night, and a ghoul was powerful enough either to kill him – or to help him in his search.

So he dismounted, took the children by the hand, washed and tidied them in a nearby stream, then unpacked his provisions, and made them eat. They were much happier little children by the time he had finished.

But suddenly they stopped in their play, and listened. Far off in the darkness someone could be heard approaching. "It is our father!" they said joyfully.

Though he was a brave hunter, Prince Ahmed didn't care to meet the ghoul-father, so he went a little way off and hid behind the trees.

The ghoul returned to his children, and was surprised to see them so clean and well-fed. "What is this?" he demanded in his grating voice.

Excitedly, the boys cried, "Prince Ahmed is here, he gave us food!"

"Come out then, Prince Ahmed," growled the ghoul, "and let's see you."

Reluctantly, Ahmed came out from behind the trees, and in the light of the fire he had lit for the children, fearfully peered at the first ghoul he had ever seen. But the ghoul kept back from the light and would not let himself be seen clearly.

At last the ghoul said, showing his white teeth in the dark, "Men who come into my domain I have for my food. I'll eat your flesh and drink your blood in one gulp!"

Prince Ahmed trembled. He knew it was no use trying to escape, because ghouls can fly. But the creature went on, "But as you have done me a good turn by caring for my boys I will promise to do you a good turn back."

"In that case," said Prince Ahmed, gaining a little courage from this answer, "I must ask you if you have seen a certain pigeon flying this way?"

The ghoul appeared to think for a moment, then said slowly, "Yes. I have seen such a bird. It left a most beautiful scent in the air."

"Then can you follow her and take me to her?" the Prince asked eagerly.

"I can, if you will provide me with seven pieces of meat and seven drinks of blood."

There was only one way in which he could provide so much meat, so he killed his horse and cut it up into seven pieces, and collected the blood into seven vessels.

"Are you ready?" asked the ghoul. "Then jump on my back and we will be off."

The ghoul flew on through the night sky for a little while, then came down to rest and demanded the first of his pieces of meat. In a great gulp he swallowed it down and asked for the blood. That too disappeared in one huge mouthful. They flew on a little further, stopped again for more meat and blood, and went on in this way until only two pieces of meat were left. As the ghoul devoured the last but one, Prince Ahmed asked him, "Is it much further now?"

"One more stop," said the ghoul gruffly, "and be sure you have that last piece of meat ready, because I'm getting tired." He took off into the air once more. Prince Ahmed clutched on to the remaining piece of meat for dear life. He seemed now to be so near his beautiful companion that he could almost feel her presence somewhere ahead.

But whether it was from being over-anxious, or whether the ghoul maliciously gave a lurch, he could not afterwards tell; but he dropped the last piece of meat.

He didn't dare tell the ghoul. But what was he to do? The ghoul would eat him if he didn't get his feast. Desperately, Prince Ahmed took out his hunting knife from his belt, and cut off a piece of his own leg, and gave it to the ghoul when he came down for his last stop.

But the ghoul knew at once he was tasting human flesh, and he laughed evilly as he chewed. He took Prince Ahmed a long, long way off, right to the second sky and finally set him down near a well over-hung by trees and bushes.

"If you wait here, your Princess's servant-girl will come sooner or later to fetch water. She will be carrying a large silver water-pot." Immediately the ghoul turned away and flew up into the air out of sight.

Prince Ahmed hid in the bushes, and waited a long time by himself. Some girls came carrying clay pots to collect the water, but none of them had a silver one, so he stayed hidden. But a girl came along who chanced to see his reflection in the water. She was so startled that she dropped her pot and broke it. She thought it was her own reflection she saw in the water, and the face was so beautiful that she said to herself, "If I am as beautiful as that, I must be a Princess myself. I will fetch and carry water no longer." Some other girls overheard her, and spread the story around.

Soon a girl came carrying a silver pot. Ahmed came out from his hiding place, and said to her, "Don't be afraid, but take this ring to your mistress and tell her I am here."

The girl went away with the ring, and spoke to her mistress. The Princess recognized the ring at once, as she had seen it often on Prince Ahmed's finger. "Bring him to me," she ordered the servant girl.

When Prince Ahmed was at last shown into the presence of his beautiful Princess, he was overcome with happiness, and poured out the story of how he had found her.

"Please, please, you must come back to me!" he pleaded.

But she said, "I will not come back with you, but you may stay with me here, on one condition."

"And what is that?"

"That you stay in the same room, and never look out of the window."

The young Prince would have promised anything so as to be near his friend, and he went with her to a fine room in her palace. There he stayed, and they saw each other every day for many months, and they were very happy together. He kept his promise not to look out of the window, for all he wanted was inside.

But there came a day when he began to feel homesick, and then he thought of looking out of the window to see where he was. "Why must I not look out of the window?" he asked himself.

Waiting until he knew the Princess would not be coming to see him for some hours, he went to the window and looked out.

Beyond the window stretched a long, wide open space. In the distance, as he looked and looked, he could see a figure. He realized it was his mother.

He could see she was preparing to sacrifice a ram, and that she was crying, and he guessed that she was doing it in the hope that God would bring her son back to her.

He determined to jump out of that window and go to her. He took a mighty leap and felt himself falling for some time, but as he fell he seemed to become lighter and lighter. At last, he landed gently in his mother's arms, to find that he was only the size of a bee.

"Well now," Halaiki said, "what do you think of the Prince called Ahmed?"

"I think he was very brave when the ghoul came through the forest like that," said Ahmed.

"Very brave! I wonder if we would all be as brave as Ahmed!" He pointed his stick at the real Ahmed, and everyone laughed.

Ahmed himself blushed. "I think I should have been very frightened," he said. "I should have run as fast as I could out of the forest." The people all laughed again, louder this time.

Halaiki held up his hands.

"No, my friends," he said, "he is right. Only a fool does not fear dangers. But listen carefully to my next story, because it is about a man who spent most of his time in fear."

Mimoun the Woodman

The land of the Middle Atlas is formed of wide steep slopes of grassland between forests of great cedar trees. In this land lived a woodman called Mimoun.

Mimoun found the work of chopping down trees and cutting up the wood very hard. It did not bring him much money. He found too that the huge trees of the forest made him afraid all the time, afraid of dark shadows that might turn out to be wild animals about to jump at him.

One day, tired from work, he sat down with his back to a tree, and he began thinking how much better life would be if he didn't have to be a woodman. Swinging his axe all day made his arms and legs and his whole body ache. When he sat down to rest, he imagined every little noise of the forest was a lion coming.

He thought the lion himself must have a very good life lazing around in his cave all day. He was so strong that every other animal ran away from him.

So Mimoun went on his knees and prayed to God to change him into a lion. A great rushing wind came driving through the forest and Mimoun got his wish. He became a lion. At once he felt his senses keener. He could see things more sharply, he could hear things more clearly, and above all his sense of smell was increased ten times. He had the powerful body of a lion, but he kept his man's brain, and thus he was truly King of the Forest.

For the whole of the following winter, he was happy. He lived in a warm cave. He hunted when he felt like it. But most of the time he lazed his days away. But when summer came, men came too. They brought sheep to the grasslands. Other men, who were hunters, came with them, to shoot lions and other animals that might attack the sheep.

The lion, who was once Mimoun the Woodman, remembered then how deadly men could be. You might easily catch one of their children – but they would seek you out and you could never beat them in the end.

So when the lion heard children shouting near his cave one day, he made a big roar and frightened them away. But he did not try to catch any of them.

Now that the children knew where he lived, they came next day to trouble him. Again he remembered how men hunt animals, with guns. He could have rushed out of his cave and killed these children easily. But he still kept the cowardly nature he had when he was Mimoun. He could picture his end coming, when maybe one bullet would wound him.

He would be helpless and the men would beat him to death.

The way to beat men was to escape from them. He crawled out of his cave another way and quickly hid behind some rocks. Sure enough the boys down below began lighting a fire at the mouth of his cave, to smoke him out. But only beetles and spiders were smoked out. He heard the boys say, "He got away this time, but we'll be back. We'll get him."

The lion in his hiding place trembled because he knew they were right.

Mimoun wished very hard to become a human again, but not as a poor woodman. He wanted to be a rich King with a golden crown on his head. And God again granted him his wish, so that the lion found himself walking through the forest as a man, with a rich golden crown on his brow.

Mimoun stepped before a very tall tree and said, "Tree! I am a King now, you must bow down before me." The tree made no reply. Mimoun shouted angrily at it, but no matter what he did nor how angry he got, the tree stood silent. Mimoun decided he must go to a town where men would know he was a King, and would bow down before him.

He walked a long, long way and he became hungry and thirsty. The heavy crown on his head was very uncomfortable, making his skin red and sweating. He took it off and covered his head with a corner of his *djellaba*. He found a small stream and stopped for a drink.

Being a King did not seem to be such a good idea after all. The rich crown only made the heat of the sun worse. Mimoun thought that only God could really do what he wanted. Perhaps if he became the sun, he would be able to lead a really happy life.

Again, his wish was granted. He became the sun. Suddenly he saw below him, as if he were a bird flying very high, the world spread out with its fields and forests, rivers and seas. He saw the deserts and mountains, all enjoying his great light. He knew he could burn them all up if he wanted, just as he had been burnt himself when he was a mere King.

But he remembered too how he had begun life in the forest and how dark it had always been down there among the trees. He thought that now he was the powerful sun, he would seek out those trees and send his light right down into them. He looked down very carefully into the earth, trying to make out the trees growing up towards him. But as fast as he picked out a forest, a black cloud slid over it and he could see nothing but grey mist. He got very angry, and decided to burn up the whole earth. The clouds just got thicker and thicker, and blacker and blacker. All his fierce heat was cooled and lost in the blowing mist.

Impatiently, he begged God to make him a cloud. He felt himself sinking down, down and down, until he had become a part of that same blanket of black cloud, covering up the sun's cruel heat and keeping it off the land. He thundered and made great zig-zag flashes of lightning, and laughed to see the people running and hiding from his rage. He laughed to see buildings struck down by his great power, big fires started by his lightning flashes. This was real power, he thought, and he was very happy to be a cloud drifting so easily over the earth.

But in a little while a tiny breeze blew up, and the breeze gathered strength and became a wind, and the wind roared and whistled and became a gale. The cloud could feel itself being torn apart. These parts then split into smaller parts, and at last the whole mass of cloud disappeared into nothing.

Mimoun thought sadly that reigning over every power there is always another power. Slowly the clouds came together again, re-forming themselves. They all complained of the mighty wind, and how he had given them so many aches and pains. He thought he would try being a wind.

Once more God granted his wish. Immediately he felt himself free and happy, chasing silly clouds about. He split them up, blew them out to sea, tore them to little pieces which the sun could dry up easily. You see, he boasted, I have to help the sun. I'm stronger than he is. At last I am happy because I am a wind. I'm so free I can go anywhere I want. I can cross seas, I can fly up over mountains. I can blow down anything that stands in my way. I can turn ships over, I can knock down houses. I can pile up the desert sands into hills and I can whistle them all flat again.

He blew at some trees in his path and tore them up by the roots. He thought of the big trees in his own village back home, tall cedar trees of immense strength. I'll go there, and show them all how strong I am, he said to himself.

So quicker than he could say it, he was off, blowing across countries and seas and islands to reach his own old village. He picked the biggest, thickest tree and gathering himself up, he blew and blew at it with all the strength he had. But the cedar tree was too firm, its trunk was wider than a man can spread his arms and its roots dug down too deep into the soil to give way. It swayed this way and that way. Its branches whipped in every direction. It creaked and groaned. But it did not fall.

"Right, my friend," said the wind, "we'll soon see who is master here." He drew back, got all his strength together once more, and returned to the attack. But the tree mocked at him.

"Go and blow the mountain snow about, little wind," it said. The wind wore himself out trying to tear up the tree. He went back up into the sky to rest and regain power. But he was very impressed with the way in which the tree had stood up to him. "The tree must be the strongest thing in all the world," he said. "How I wish I was a tree like that one down there."

At once the wind felt himself spinning round and round so fast that he became dizzy and dived into the ground below. Immediately he grew up into an immensely tall tree. He could feel his roots reaching right down into the soil till he was able to coil them round the very rock beneath the soil. "Nothing can beat me now," he said proudly, and he had many good battles with the wind.

He was truly happy being a tree. He lost a branch or two now and then, but the winds never beat him. The forest was peaceful and he could see the earth properly. No gales, snowstorms nor the hot sun itself could do anything to him. He thought, I have even beaten time, because a tree lives for hundreds of years. Each night as dark closed over the forest, he slept more contentedly than he had ever done before.

But one morning he woke up with a terrible ache

in his trunk low down near the ground. The ache got worse. It became a pain that got sharper and sharper.

What was this pain, do you think?

It was a woodman's axe. It bit steadily into the tree's strong trunk. Soon he felt himself toppling over, with a long way to fall on to a big rock below. In despair, he prayed to God to make him a woodman again.

But in Mimoun's mind the tree never hit the rock. He had been dreaming. He woke up in his own forest, close to his own village.

Trembling still from the fright of being chopped down by the woodman's axe, Mimoun immediately went down on his knees, and begged God's pardon for his pride and his grumbling, which had made him wish to be all these different things. He promised God he would accept himself as he was now. A poor, hard-working, not very brave woodman. After all, he thought, a hard-working man is the strongest creature on this earth.

After this Mimoun became a happier man. The same year he got married to a girl of his village, and they had many children who would one day help him in his work as a woodman.

"We have heard much of the troubles of mankind," said Halaiki after he had brought the story of Mimoun to an end. "Tomorrow let me tell you about the problems of the wolf who lost his tail."

Ahmed paid his money and ran home as usual, and was in good time for supper.

But the next afternoon, as he walked quietly along the balcony above his father's head, he dropped one of his sandals. It slid over the edge and landed right in his father's lap below.

"Ahmed!" called his father at once. "Is that you? Where are you going?"

Ahmed looked over the rail of the balcony. "I . . . I was going for a walk."

"But this is the time you should be studying?"

"Yes, father, but . . ."

"No 'buts'. Go back to your room."

Unhappily, Ahmed went back and sat down on his bed. But a minute or two later he heard his father leave the courtyard. Quickly he made his way down to the street door, and ran all the way to the Djemaa el Fna on bare feet.

He arrived just in time, panting, as Halaiki was beginning.

The Hedgehog and the Wolf

A vineyard lay on the slopes of a mountain of the Atlas, not far from here. It was full of tempting ripe grapes. The farmer had built a wall round it, but a hole had been made in this wall, and one day through the hole came creeping a hedgehog and a wolf. The farmer was asleep in the noonday sun, so the two friends were able to eat as many grapes as they could manage.

The hedgehog, though, was a little worried that he would not be able to get out again, so he kept on trying himself in the hole, to see if he could still fit inside it. But the wolf just ate and ate and ate the lovely grapes, and then licked the sweet juice that ran down his jaws.

Even lazy farmers wake up sooner or later, and when they heard him coming the two animals dashed in a panic for their hole. The hedgehog easily squeezed through, but for the wolf it was hopeless from the start. He had eaten far too many grapes.

His friend hissed advice to him from the other side. "Lie down and play dead. That's right! Roll over on your back, legs in the air. Good! Don't move a muscle!"

"Hah-hah-hah!" roared the farmer angrily, seeing the wolf. "So you thought you'd steal my grapes, did you? Well, I've got you now! But what's this? Dead, are you? Eaten too many? Serves you right, then. Well, I'll not have dead wolves lying in my vineyard."

So he picked up the wolf by the tail, whirled him round and round his head until he got up a great speed and threw him over the wall. No sooner did the wolf feel his feet on the ground than he ran off as fast as he could go.

The farmer shouted after him. "All right! You tricked me that time, but I'll get you. I'll know who you are next time!"

The wolf looked back over his shoulder, and to his horror saw the farmer waving a big grey tail in his hand. The tail had come right off and in his dizziness after being whirled around he had not felt it.

Finding his friend the hedgehog a little way off, the wolf said in despair, "What am I to do now? The farmer will know me because a wolf without a tail is a marked animal."

The hedgehog looked at him thoughtfully for a moment. "Never mind," he said at last. "Leave it to me. I'll fix it up for you."

A day or two later, the wolf was surprised to be asked to a party the hedgehog was giving. When he got there, it was to find that the other guests were all wolves, much like himself.

"Now," said the hedgehog, "we're all going to play a game first."

"Oh, yes," said the wolves, "let's play a game. What game do you suggest, hedgehog?"

"We'll play a game called Milling the Corn. You all have your tails tied to this millstone, and then you try to get it moving round till you are all running very fast." He pointed to a large, heavy millstone he had on the ground outside his door.

"Oh, marvellous," they all said. "We like running round. We're good at that."

So the hedgehog arranged them in a circle, and carefully tied the tail of each wolf to the millstone. He stood back and said, "Ready? Go!"

The wolves all tugged and pulled very hard, and slowly the huge round stone began to turn. They yelled with delight and pulled all the harder. Soon they were rushing round at a fine rate. The wolf who had lost his tail didn't play. He just sat looking on, thinking sadly it looked a very good game if one only had a tail.

Suddenly the hedgehog shouted at the top of his voice, "The hunters are coming, my friends! Run for your lives!" At the same time he banged a tin with a stick he had behind his back.

The wolves were frightened out of their wits, and leapt away so suddenly that each and every one of their tails came off. The tails lay on the ground, still firmly tied to the millstone.

"Come back!" shouted the hedgehog to his friend, who had been as terrified as the rest. "There aren't really any hunters."

The wolf came back panting. "No hunters?" he gasped, his mouth hanging open.

"No, there are no hunters," said the hedgehog, smiling. "But there are now ten wolves without tails!"

"Now think to yourselves," Halaiki said, "are you hedgehogs or wolves?"

"The wolf was very stupid," said Ahmed. "I wouldn't want to be like him. But . . ."

"But you don't like to say you'd be as clever as the hedgehog, eh? That's good. It's a foolish man who boasts." He looked at the sky. "You were late coming tonight, Ahmed. Was anything wrong?"

"My father caught me leaving the house, and he said I must read my schoolbooks."

"Quite right too. Schoolbooks are important. But you got away?"

"Yes," said Ahmed, "but I don't know what I'm going to say when my father asks me about my lessons."

Halaiki smiled. "Then I will tell you a story about a boy who was very clever at his schoolwork. But strange to tell, his *father wished he had not been so clever."*

Shafiq the Sailor

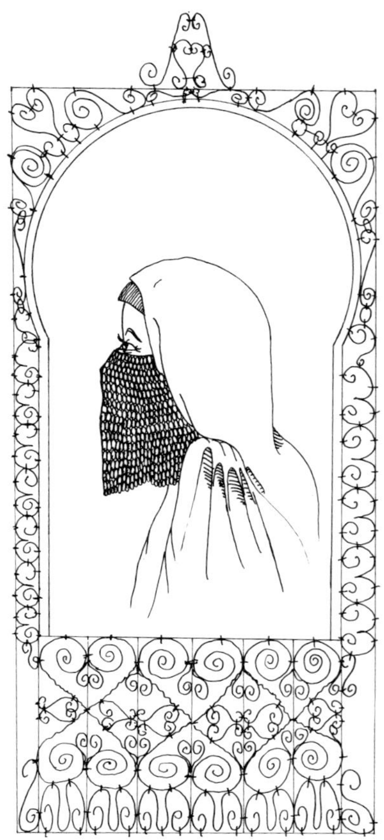

THE FIRST VOYAGE

In one of the great seaports of our country, there once lived a successful merchant. When he was a young man, without money or education, he had worked very hard and made enough money to fit out a small ship. He had filled this ship with all kinds of good things and had set out to trade with anyone he could find. He had bought his goods wisely, and he sold them at a fine profit.

With this profit, he had fitted out a larger ship, and went to sea as before, to sell his goods. Each time he returned home he was a little richer. Each time he set sail again, it was with a larger ship, then two ships, then three. He became very rich, and he was well known in that seaport for his successful trading. He had one fault, and that was that he had rather a quick temper.

This merchant was blessed with a fine son named Shafiq. He wanted Shafiq to follow him in his business. But he thought, as he was now rich, that Shafiq should go to school and learn all the things that clever men knew. He himself had never had time for school.

So Shafiq spent his boyhood studying with clever teachers and learning the mysteries of this world. He was an intelligent boy, and did well with his teachers. His father was careful not to trouble him with business matters until he was twenty-one. Then he called him to his room, and said, "Shafiq, my son, you have done well in your studies, and I am pleased with you. Now with this fine education, you will be able to talk to clever men anywhere in the world. I am sure you will do better in life than ever your poor old father did."

Shafiq was a modest and kind young man, who loved his father, so he said, "Well, father, I shall do my best, but everyone knows what a clever merchant you are. I shall have to do very well indeed to be more successful than you."

His father was pleased with this answer and

replied, "Shafiq, you must now learn how to do business. You may know about the moon and the stars, and about far countries, and you may know all the wisdom in the great books our forefathers wrote." He smiled at his son, and putting a hand on his shoulder to show he did not mean his next words unkindly, he went on, "But I don't believe you could sell water in the desert, or salt to a cook. You will have to start from the beginning. I am going to fit out a ship for you, fill it with goods, and you shall set sail and see how you get on."

The ship was made ready, and every kind of merchandise was put into it, all of the best quality and the most tempting variety to attract buyers. The merchant went down to the quay to see his son off and give him his blessing. Shafiq was very excited, and he was sure that he would come back rich. But his father, waving his handkerchief high in the air as the ship got smaller and smaller out at sea, had his doubts. "My poor Shafiq," he muttered to himself, "a good, clever, honest boy. But couldn't sell a file to a man in jail. Allah, Allah, oh Lord God Allah, have I done the right thing?" But it was too late now. When he looked up, the ship was gone.

For several days, Shafiq sailed over blue seas watching everything that came his way with the greatest interest and enthusiasm. Flying fish landed on his deck, and he remembered what his teacher had told him about these curious creatures. They passed islands, and he noted what kind of trees grew there, and how the people built their boats.

One day, they saw another ship sailing towards them. As it came nearer, Shafiq could hear screams and cries of pain. He commanded his crew to sail near the other ship, and he called out to the Captain, "Are you in trouble? Can we help you?"

The Captain came to the deck-rail of his vessel and shouted back, "No, thank you. We're all right. What you hear is the slaves I'm carrying."

"Slaves?" said Shafiq. "What are you doing with slaves?"

"I'm taking them to sell them," replied the Captain.

"May I see them?" asked Shafiq.

The Captain said of course he could see them, and invited him aboard his ship. So Shafiq was rowed across and climbed up into the strange vessel. The Captain showed him around, and Shafiq was very unhappy to see the poor slaves in chains, with the marks of the whip on their backs. Some of them looked up at him so piteously that he said to his host, "You say you're selling them? How much do you want?"

The Captain looked at him for a moment, then asked, "What can you offer?"

"My ship is loaded with goods for trading," said Shafiq. He thought, what are a few rugs and copper pans beside the happiness of these suffering people?

"Well, suppose we do an exchange?" said the

crafty Captain, eyeing the fine ship that Shafiq's father had had fitted out for him. He thought that the cargo must certainly be of more value than his slaves.

"Very well," said Shafiq, longing to get his sailors to strike off the chains from the slaves' legs.

So they exchanged cargoes and the Captain sailed away as quick as he could find a wind.

Shafiq freed all the slaves and watched them stretch their cramped limbs on his deck. But when he heard where each one came from, he determined to take his ship and return all of them to their homes.

They had a long voyage, going from port to port and leaving the slaves one by one in their home countries. At last, all were put ashore but one young girl and her nurse. This girl was very beautiful and Shafiq felt very sorry for her. She said she had no home and would like to return to his country to see if anyone would employ her and her old nurse. Shafiq agreed at once.

On the voyage back to his father's homeland, Shafiq found himself more and more attracted to the young girl. He said to her, "You do not need to find a job. Marry me instead."

The girl agreed and the young couple were very happy.

By this time, the father was very worried about his son and his ship. By his reckoning, they should have been back long before this. He was afraid they might have been wrecked. Every day he stood on the harbour walls and searched the horizon

anxiously for any signs of a sail. Each one that came into view he examined eagerly until he could see it was not his ship.

Then at last Shafiq came sailing back home. His father could see from the state of the once new ship that they must have had a very long voyage. He hoped that meant everything was sold and his son was now a rich man.

But Shafiq jumped down on to the quay in a torn and dirty robe. He looked very thin.

His father saw these things but held his arms wide in welcome. "My dear son! Back safe at last! Tell me, tell me everything. But why are you so poorly dressed and thin?"

"Father," said Shafiq. "I have good and bad news. Which shall I tell you first?"

The merchant put an anxious hand to his heart, and said, fearing the worst, "The bad, my boy, the bad first."

So Shafiq explained about the slaves and the exchange he had done with the Captain. He and his sailors had had to give their spare clothes to the slaves. The extra long voyage they had made, together with all the extra mouths, meant that there had been very little to eat in the last days.

"But Father," pleaded Shafiq, "if you could have seen those poor people, you would have done the same."

His father looked at him, quite speechless. He said after a long silence, "And the goods I gave you? All gone?"

Shafiq nodded.

"Not one dinar in return?"

Shafiq shook his head.

"You booby!" burst out the old merchant, losing his temper. "You great camel-witted booby! *I* would have done the same? Oh you miserable scraping of a dirty dish! How dare you say it? There's no more brains in you than a pail of curdled goatsmilk! I knew you couldn't sell a feather to a plucked chicken!" He stopped for breath then said, as a tiny last hope, "You brought *nothing* back, absolutely nothing?"

"Well," said Shafiq, more cheerfully, "that's the good news. Here is my future wife." And he turned and called to the girl who, while this was going on, still waited in the ship.

Despite the terrible shock he had had at his son's adventure, the old merchant couldn't help being delighted with her – she was so good and beautiful. He calmed down a little, and greeted the girl kindly and they all went to his house to rest and eat. But the father said, "Never again! No more ships or trading for you, you empty orange-skin of a youth!"

Shafiq and the girl were married and were very happy with one another. The merchant thought and and thought what was the best thing to do with his son. The more he thought, the more he felt like forgiving him. "After all," he said to himself, "he is young. It is a good thing to feel sorry for people when you are young. Perhaps he didn't do so badly. He will learn."

So in the end he did forgive Shafiq, and decided to let him try again.

The old man stopped, and took out his collecting bag. "We must continue the story tomorrow, my friends. I am tired now."

To Ahmed, he said, "I hope you can come tomorrow to hear the rest of the story."

"I hope so too," said Ahmed, but all the way home he was wondering what he would say to his father.

At the supper table, his father said, "Ahmed, I hope you did your work well this evening."

Ahmed stayed silent, looking down at his food.

"Come along, my son," said his father kindly, "tell me what you learned."

Still, Ahmed could find nothing to say.

His father frowned, "Did you go out after all? After I told you to go to your room?"

Ahmed nodded.

His father looked sternly at him for a long time. At last, he said, "You must learn obedience, my son. Tomorrow, there will be no going out. If you have not learned your lessons, you will be punished."

Here was a terrible thing! If he stayed in, he would never know what happened to Shafiq. But if he went out . . .!

Ahmed slept badly that night, and all next day he wondered if his father's punishment would be very bad. But as the drums began to beat that afternoon, he simply could not let Shafiq end his adventures without being there to hear.

He slipped out as usual, being especially careful not to drop his sandals, and took his place before the man in the circle.

THE SECOND VOYAGE

A new ship was made ready. Some of the best goods from the old merchant's warehouse were put into it. For the second time, the father came to see his son off.

"This time," he said, "keep away from all other ships. Make sure you land at a rich port, where you can sell everything for the best prices. Don't worry about your wife, we'll look after her well."

As he waved at the ship's sail, far out to sea, he muttered to himself, "Allah, I hope I did right to give him a second chance. As you are kind and merciful to true believers, so it must be a good thing for Shafiq to be kind and merciful too. Allah, you will watch over him, I know, and reward an old man."

This time he did not say anything more to Allah, but to himself he thought, the booby couldn't sell a frown to a tax-gatherer!

Shafiq and his faithful crew sailed on and on over the blue sea, passing many other ships on the way. But Shafiq was ashamed that he had lost all his good father's money on the first voyage. He carefully obeyed his father's wishes, and did not try to hail any of them. At last, they came to a great city at the other side of the sea. Shafiq ordered his men to put into the port, and eagerly he looked forward to doing rich trade.

But when they had tied the ship up to one of the quays, they could find no one about. They walked into the city a little way, and what should they see but crowds of people being dragged along the streets by soldiers with sticks and whips. Little children were running along, crying, after their mothers and fathers.

Shafiq had some trouble in finding someone who would explain what was happening. But when he did, he was told that these were poor people who could not afford to pay the high taxes demanded by the King of that country.

"Is that all?" said Shafiq. "For that, they get beaten and put in prison? What a cruel man the King must be."

He went back to his ship, found some merchants of that place, and sold all his goods. Then he went

back to the soldiers he had seen before, and offered to pay the taxes for the poor people. The soldiers thought him mad, but took the money and let the people go.

The ship was now empty and there was nothing to do but sail back home again. Shafiq realised that he had failed his father for the second time.

When they got home, his father couldn't believe it. This time at least they still had their clothes, and some of the food they had taken with them was left over. So he thought Shafiq was playing a joke on him.

"Ha! So you're teasing your old father, you heartless boy? Really you have seven chests full of gold, haven't you? Ha, Ha! A good joke. But remember, don't joke like that again. Any more shocks like last time, and I couldn't stand it. I should drop dead on the spot. Now, let's see this lovely gold!"

When he found that the ship contained nothing but empty boxes, and that Shafiq had not been joking, he flew into an awful rage.

"You giddy-head! You thick-skull! You . . . you hoddy-doddy! What have you done this time? No, don't tell me I would have done the same! I'll kill you! Oh that I should live to see my son such a witless mooncalf! You couldn't sell a banana to a starving monkey! You couldn't . . . you couldn't . . ."

But the old fellow had so run himself out of breath that he had to sit down. Shafiq stood there not knowing what to do. At last his father, his rage gone, said, "No, never again, and this time I mean it. It's more than I can stand. You and your wife get out of my house! I won't see you ever again."

So poor Shafiq and his wife were thrown out of the merchant's house. They went to take refuge with a kind friend of Shafiq's.

The kind friend knew the old merchant well. He knew his rages were very bad, but they did not last long. He said to Shafiq, "Do nothing. Stay here for a while, and soon I will go to your father, and see if he will give you another chance."

THE THIRD VOYAGE

This man did speak to the father, who forgot his rage and agreed to make a third ship ready. But this time he thought of a way of making sure the young man remembered what he must do. He had a fine picture of Shafiq's wife painted. This picture he hung up in Shafiq's cabin on the ship. When he came to say goodbye once more, he gave him his blessing and said, "Now see. There is the likeness of your wife. Look at that picture every day, and remember. If you don't come back with gold in exchange for your goods this time, she will suffer. Never mind slaves and people who can't pay their taxes. Your own wife will suffer. I promise you."

Shafiq promised faithfully that he would look at his wife's picture every day, and he would be very, very careful this time. He and his sailors set the sail, and were off once more.

The father muttered, "Oh great Allah, this time he has learned his lesson. This time he will succeed.

I know that if I say he couldn't sell a rope to a drowning man, you will prove me wrong."

Shafiq guided his ship a new way, and after a long voyage put in at a port belonging to a great Emperor of those times. He did not dare to go into the city in case he saw something that would lead him astray from his business, as had happened before. So he leaned over the rail of his ship and called to the merchants on the quay to come and buy his goods.

After some time, a richly dressed man came on board and inspected the colourful rugs and rich clothes and other things Shafiq's father had sent for trading. He bought many things and Shafiq was very pleased that at last he had done what he came for.

They went to his cabin to complete their bargain. The rich man saw the picture of Shafiq's wife. He studied it for a moment and asked, "Tell me, who is that lady?"

"She is my wife," Shafiq said proudly.

"Is it a good likeness?" asked the merchant.

"Very good. Why do you ask?"

"Because it looks like . . . a lady I know. Wait here, my friend, I'll be back."

The man went away, leaving Shafiq to wonder what new mystery this might be. But soon a party of horsemen came riding down to the harbour, escorting not only the merchant, but the Emperor of the city as well.

The Emperor came on board, and was taken down to the cabin to see the picture of Shafiq's wife. As soon as he set eyes on it, his face changed.

He smiled and gazed in wonder at it by turns. At last, he said to Shafiq, "Young man, this is a picture of my daughter. I sent her away many months ago for disobeying me. But I have forgiven her long since, and have been wondering where she went. Now it seems she is your wife."

"That is true, Your Majesty," said Shafiq, and he told the Emperor the story of how he had rescued her from the slave Captain.

The Emperor was delighted to know she was safe, and he asked Shafiq to sail home and fetch her, and to bring his own family too, so that they could all be happy together.

As you can imagine, Shafiq lost no time setting sail for home. Very long did the days seem before he came in sight of the old harbour, with his father sitting waiting for him.

This time his father had no complaints. A few days later the whole party set out to make the voyage to the Emperor's Kingdom.

Now it chanced that the Emperor had sent one of his ministers back with Shafiq to accompany his only child back to her rightful home. This man had thought deeply about what Shafiq's coming might mean, and he had become jealous of him. He thought he would see to it that Shafiq never arrived in the Emperor's Court. So one dark night on board ship, he waited his chance, and pushed Shafiq overboard.

No one heard any cries for help and in the morning when it was found that Shafiq was missing, there was very much grief on the ship. They turned round and searched for several hours but in the end they had to give up and sail on to tell the Emperor the terrible news.

Meanwhile, Shafiq struggled for his life in the sea. He swam and swam till he was quite exhausted, but came in sight of a lonely rock. He managed to climb out of the water and find a resting place. But when he had recovered enough strength to explore the little island, he found it was completely bare. Nothing grew there. There was no sight of any other land. Shafiq saw he was no better off than before. He would starve to death.

Some days went by, and Shafiq grew weak. On the third day, a small boat came in sight, and Shafiq waved his arms till the sailor saw him and came up to the rock. It was an old fisherman. The man looked at Shafiq with amazement, and asked how he came to be there. He explained how he had nearly been drowned, and told him about the jealous minister.

The old man realized that Shafiq must be an important person. So he said, "I'm only a poor fisherman. What will you give me if I rescue you?"

Desperately, Shafiq said, "Anything. Anything."

"Very well," said the fisherman, "you must promise to give me half of anything you get in the future."

Shafiq promised to do this, and so was taken off the rock. He had a long and weary journey before he could come again to the Emperor's Kingdom.

Great was the joy when he was united with his wife and his father. The old man clasped his son in his arms, and muttered, "Not such a jolter-head after all!"

"How did you come to fall overboard?" asked the wife.

Shafiq explained how he had been pushed by the minister. "But," he said earnestly. "I do not want you to have him punished."

"What!" said the old father, beginning to lose his temper. "Not punish such a wicked man! You're a lackwit, a driveller! An eater of dried-out asses' tails!"

"No," said Shafiq, "the unhappy man thought I

should take his place in the Emperor's palace. I don't blame him for feeling jealous."

"Oh Allah! but he nearly drowned you! He intended to, anyway, didn't he? That I should have such a ninny for a son! First he gives away my treasure for a few miserable slaves. Then it's peasants who can't pay taxes! Now he forgives a murderer! What will he do next?"

"You're forgetting that one of those miserable slaves was an Emperor's daughter!" laughed Shafiq. "Besides," he went on, "forgiveness is a great virtue, Father, and in any case I have learned it from you. You have forgiven me twice, have you not?"

His father, for once, had nothing to say to this.

The Emperor also thought forgiveness was a virtue. When his daughter told him the whole story, he said, "Your husband is a wise man as well as kind, my dear. He shall be Emperor after me."

Shafiq's father cooled down, as he always did, and they all lived contentedly in that kingdom for many years.

But at last the Emperor died, and Shafiq became Emperor in his place.

As he went before the people to be proclaimed the new Emperor, a voice was heard above the noise of the crowd.

"Oh Emperor Shafiq! Remember your promise to the old fisherman!"

Shafiq recognized the old man who had saved him from the lonely rock.

His old father, now bent and white-haired, stepped forward and shouted, "Away with him! Seize him, guards. What insolence!"

But Shafiq said, "No, let him approach. Now, what was it I promised you, old man?"

"You promised me one half of whatever you gained in future."

"Madness!" shouted the father. "A noodle Emperor! A babbler! A looby dolt!"

But Shafiq did not listen. He led the fisherman to his treasury, and said, smiling, "Take half, old man! I promised it, and there is plenty there."

And so began the rule of the Emperor Shafiq, one of the best and wisest Emperors ever to rule over that country.

But at times visitors to the Court would hear an old, old man wandering about the Palace muttering, "Couldn't sell a needle to a tailor! The booby! Couldn't even sell a coffin to a dead man!"

The Djemaa el Fna grew dark as Halaiki ended his story of Shafiq. He took out his bag and went round the circle collecting money.

Everyone liked the story, and the bag was already quite fat as he came to Ahmed. The boy put in his coin, and stood up slowly.

Halaiki looked at him with a smile in his eyes. "You are very quiet, Ahmed. Did you again come without your father's permission?"

"Yes," answered Ahmed. He smiled back. "But I think I know now what I will say to him."

"That is good," said the old man, "then go with Allah."

Ahmed ran home, went into the house, and sat down at his place just in time for the family supper.

His father seemed to be in a good mood. He smiled at his son, and said, "Have you learned many useful things today, Ahmed?"

"Yes, father, I have. But first, I'd like to tell you a story."

"A story?" his father said, looking around the room. "I'm sure we all like stories. What is this one about?"

"Well . . ." said Ahmed, slowly. "It's about – about an old father and his clever son."

"Oh, is it?" was the answer. "Let us hear it then."

Ahmed began, "In one of the great seaports of our country, there once lived a successful merchant . . ." and he told them the story of Shafiq the Sailor.

The family was still sitting over the empty dishes when Ahmed came to the end of it.

They had all laughed a lot at the old father, and Ahmed had looked secretly at his own father as he told the story.

Now his father said, "You didn't learn that story from a schoolbook!"

"No, I learned it from Halaiki," said Ahmed truthfully.

His father looked at him, but he did not seem to be angry. He said, "Shafiq was very silly, giving away all that money."

"Yes, but father, if he hadn't given away his cargo in exchange for the slaves, he would never have married the Emperor's daughter. And if he hadn't . . ."

"Yes, yes, I see all that. But remember, the old merchant himself would never have given away such a rich cargo for just a few slaves. Do you think Shafiq would have done so, if he had not had that good education? Think about that, Ahmed, next time you want to laugh at your old father's advice!"